The Colors of Love
Poetry of The Crimson Spirit

Jaumonta Roberts

WARNING
Adult Content Within

The Colors of Love: Poetry of The Crimson Spirit

For all those who have ever loved under the rainbow

This book of prose is dedicated to all of you. Do not feel ashamed
to love as you do or to love who you do.
~We are all facets' of the same prism, shinning bright and bending
colors from our given and eternal light~

CONTENTS

ACKNOWLEDGMENTS

I first want to give thanks to my mother, Julieana who has always allowed me to discover my own way, my father, Jacques who I love, my brother, Jarrett and sister, Jaunae to whom I hope to one day give the world. Your brother truly loves you more than you know. A loving thanks to my grandmother Joanetta, we would all not be here if not for you. I could not forget three of my favorite aunts. My aunt Jovana, you have always offered your time and your heart to me. My aunt Angelia, you never failed whenever I needed you most. I hope to one day be able to return that favor. Also my aunt Jillinda, who is my birthday twin, I love you so much. Thank you to all my family and friends for all of your support in any capacity, I love you all.

And a special thanks to my eighth grade English teacher Salome DeShay, she was the catalyst to my poetic influence, after her many others fanned the flames of my poetic script, of those individuals I would also like to thank Michelle Carey, Lena Cole Dennis, Angela N. Parker, Donna Derden and Kori Williams.

For Chris, James, Ronya, Toby & Willie
Who will forever be missed, but never forgotten

My poetry is NOT an obsession; it's more like a possession.
Where the paper meets the pen, the words pour out from the
soul within and with that said let us begin...

1. "No More Lies"

Some live a life of unknown trust
Some live a life of which they must
No more lies living in your head
No more lies hiding up under your bed

Keep the truth living in your heart
And you will be off to a beautiful start
Let the word of God set you free
And keep the Devil crying on his knees
More can be said and much to be done
About the word that must be sung

No more lies causing you trouble
No more lies leaving you in the rubble
Be good to yourself and be good to others
Let love & joy be to all your mothers

Don't go around making problems
Work them out and try to solve them
No more lies keeping you out of the light
No more lies causing you to end your life

By: **The Crimson Spirit (T.C.S.)**

circa 1995

This poem was the first of many that poured out of my heart once the flood gates of prose was released in me during my high school English class. After reciting this poem in different circles at different points in my life, blindly unaware of its "true" meaning; I finally realized that this poem was my hearts first truth and its first attempt at self acceptance. It saddened me to realize that I had been living a lie for so many years and the fear of discovery or rejection once the truth was known was weighing on me heavily.

It was still a few years later before I trusted my family with my secret. I had family members that were close to my age at the time and they never questioned how I loved and accepted me as I was, but they were not my life's true critics. I dreaded the thought of telling the older members of my family, especially my mother about how I felt and loved for fear of her response or her blaming herself for what I was discovering myself to be. It was a close friend at the time who told me that I had to tell my mother to release myself from the fear of discovery.

He made it seem so simple, "Once you tell your mother, it won't matter what anyone else has to say. She brought you in this world and whether she accepts you or not. No one can hurt her by telling her before you get the chance to tell her in your own words". This was on the night of a release party for a gay magazine that I was featured in. The article was titled "Young, Gifted & Gay"; my friend was even more amazed that I would allow the world to view me as "gay" before I was even capable of telling my own mother. His words sat with me for days before I chickened out and purposely dropped a copy of the magazine in her car one day when she dropped me off.

It wasn't long after we parted before the house phone started blowing up. I believe I avoided her first call. Then there were four more calls back to back. I remember feeling as if my walls were on the verge of crumbling down and I was going to be left unshielded from an assault that I spent most of my life avoiding. When I finally answered, she did not seem too annoyed, but more skeptical than anything else. This provided some relief for me. I still kept my conversation with her short cause I wasn't really prepared to go into any long drawn out details about my emerging sex life right away.

Needless to say, things between us eventually normalized and as for the rest of the family, since I started with my mother I just figured that from her the information would just trickle down to everyone else. I started to "act" as if they all knew about my sexuality. We are all better than ever now and I am forever grateful to the friend who inspired me to allow my family into this most guarded secret about my life.

2. "The Life of a Poem"

When a man sits down with
a pen
His heart and mind
become open
As he lifts his hand
to write
Words pour out, as if
in flight
With twist and turns
they rhyme
Making a poem
in time
The poem is then
shown around
If it is good, it may
leave town
With time the poem
moves along
Bringing hope, peace and love with a
beautiful song
In time the poet
is gone
But his words in the poem
live on
The poem is read, copied
and examined
Now it has
become demanded
The poem in itself
becomes famous
Leaving behind a poet who
remained nameless

By: **The Crimson Spirit (T.C.S.)**
© 1995

While sitting in class one afternoon, looking over my first bunch of poems, a classmate told me that I did not write all those (referring to my small collection of poetry). It was the first time anyone had challenged my validity as an aspiring poet. I was not prepared by any means, but could not allow him to attempt to extinguish my inner fire for poetry before it even had a chance to burn. So while he watched I scribbled out this poem that I feel truly depicts what some artist leave in their legacy... an anonymous yet autonomous and powerful movement that exists long after they are dead and gone, never knowing all the lives they touched, changed and inspired.

This is not what I wanted for my poetry. I want to be known while I'm still here and able to address any questions or criticisms of my work. I want to remove the need or reason to misinterpret what my poetry meant or represents.

Many of my poems are based on my life experiences in love or my interpretation of things I have witnessed real or imagined in dreams. It's funny to me in hindsight how many of my poems are about love and also knowing that the bulk of them in the beginning were not factual love, but the imagining of love being reciprocated by a high school crush.

To this day I still have dreams of what my life would have been like with my crush if I were: 1) born a girl and was afforded the option to marry this man, or 2) if I was able to love this man openly and completely as only another man can. To this day he is still a very close friend and cherished component of my life, I have told him how I feel, he is just unable to reciprocate love in the ways I have for all these years dreamed of.

Alas, love still eludes this faithful, honest, loving spirit of the universe.

3. "Motherhood"

To be a mother is a gift from above
and not for what you're thinking of

A mother must go through a trial & error phase
Until she knows that child's way
With love and trust that must be obeyed
Is very needed for that child to behave

Time goes on, the child now older
His conflicts now becomes bolder and bolder
After a time when he moves on,
His mother will look back on times now gone

A mother must go through a trial & error phase
Until she knows her son knows his way

With a smile and grin
She tells her friends of the times she & her son have spent
A voice full of wisdom and spice,
tells friends of how her son was anything, but nice

To be a mother is a love from above
To show her that she is loved

In a time that could not be foretold
The mother gets visits from her sons' children, young & old
The stories she tells, makes them laugh and giggle
Of how in church their father would squirm & wiggle

As you can see a mother's job is never done
She sings a song all mothers have sung
Motherhood is a wonderful thing

Jaumonta Roberts

Please don't treat it as just another fling

To be a mother takes a special love,
that can only be given from mother to son

By: **The Crimson Spirit (T.C.S.)**
circa 1995
Rev. November 2012

-Inspired by the love between a single mother and son

Thinking back to a time when the poetry bug first bit me. I remember writing a poem every day for a week straight. One of those poems was this one "Motherhood", which was written around mother's day as a class assignment. After writing the first draft, I was inspired during editing to revise it three different ways, ending up with four version of the same poem. Over the years I misplaced the other versions and was only left with this one. Then I later on recalled a line from "Sister Act 2: Back in the Habit", "If you wake up in the morning, and you can't think of anything but singing first, then you supposed to be a singer, girl."After that recollection, I still was not fully convinced though. I chalked it all up to be a fluke or something that would never pan out into anything greater. Now here it is many years later and I see how wrong I truly was.

4. "Life on a Dead-end Street"

My life is running on a dead-end street
More and more cars trying to make me feel the heat

It's hard trying to keep up the pace
When cars keep slinging mud in your face

You can't get a job to save your life
When cars hold you back with all their might

Sleeping on the edge is hard indeed
When so many cars are dying for speed

Drive-bys, sirens, and barking dogs, your alarm clocks
Jail bars, old cars, condemned buildings, your safe locks

The dangers of living on a dead-end street
You don't know who's bringing your next feast

Rats, cats, dogs, mice your entrees
Next day, cars calling for strays

Living on the streets you must keep on your toes
If you get killed, nobody knows

Staying in shelters is a part of your life
Police controlling the on and off of the lights

Sleeping with your bag under your head
Sleeping with your shoes tied under your bed

Morning comes, back on the street
Not knowing the next place you're going to eat

Washing windows and shining shoes
Is the only way to pay your dues

You're tired, you're weary, you cannot stand up
Cars go by calling you a drunk

Crossing the street, you fall to your knees
Knowing this is the last time you'll ever say, "Please..."

You lift your head to the sky as you lose consciousness
Knowing that you have now drawn your very last breath

You're taken away, no autopsy needed
Now you're in the closet cemetery

A hole is dug, you're flung inside
Without a tombstone by the graveside

By: **The Crimson Spirit (T.C.S.)**
circa 1995

-Inspired by the movie "The Saint of Fort Washington" (1993)-

I can't remember now too much about this movie, but I do remember being so moved by its plot that the following morning right after waking, the words just poured out of me. It was on this day that I realized that I was truly bitten by the poetry bug.

After performing the piece for different audiences around Los Angeles, I was offered places to stay, shelter resources and financial donations. All of which I gracefully declined after explaining that I have never been homeless, but was just deeply inspired.

Looking back over my life now though I realize for many years I WAS homeless. Not living on the streets though, but just not having a permanent residence to call my own. I have been blessed though to have great friends and family who loved and kept me sheltered (sleeping on couches and sharing spare rooms) for most of my life. Recently I have acquired my own residence and the peace of mind that comes along with it.

5. "Slave to Love For U"

Seeing your face everywhere I go
Listening to your voice in every love song I know
Admiring your face when it is without dismay
Void is the feeling I feel when you're away
Enveloped in your love like an un-grown seed

To wrap your body within my arms is all I need
Open your heart free willing to me

Lover, to you that's what I'll be
Over and over you turn my life around
Very smooth fingers keep me from feeling down
Embracing the thought of being your one and only

Forever and always you will never be lonely
On my way to your house I keep a steady pace
Reminded always of being within your warm embrace

Understand my love for you is sweeter than honeydew
and no one can love me like you

By: **The Crimson Spirit (T.C.S.)**
circa 1995

-This is one of my first poetry challenges to myself-

This poem was my first attempt at spelling out the title of the poem in the actual poem. When I tell other poets about this, many tell me that for them the poem comes first then the title. I have always seemed to be able to write a title and the poem pours out from that focal point and by the time I reach the bottom of the page, the poem is completed. It's been years since I challenged myself to a writing style. Maybe it's time to think of something new to do?

Sometimes my poetry challenges fail, but other times great poems prevail.

6. "My Friend"

My friend is leaving
My feelings are deceiving
My eyes see happiness
My heart feels sadness
My ears hear joy
My mind is a void
My mouth says good-bye
My eyes begin to cry
My mind thinks this to be fake
My hands start to shake

I really don't believe this to be true, but I don't want this to
happen to any of you
I never expected to lose a friend this dear, just thinking
about it brings forth a tear
Being without my friend will be such a pain, that only
intensifies during the mid-night rain
The sound of laughter from others drives me insane, does
anyone else feel this pain
My friend is leaving, there is nothing left to say. Only one
thing is on my mind and that's

STAY!

By: **The Crimson Spirit (T.C.S.)**
© 1997

7. "For a Friend"

Pain is what I feel

Hate remains still

No more jokes that we can share

No more smiles, cause you're not there

I'm crying

Wish I were dying

My heart burns with fire

While your spirit rises higher

Wish you were here with me

Only now you're sailing on a silver sea

You should be happy, wish you could tell

I should be happy for you, cause you left this world of Hell

No more tears for you to cry

No more need to say "good-bye"

Your son and daughter, let them be strong

For they loved you their whole life long

This poem has now come to an end

But I will never forget you, my friend

By: **The Crimson Spirit (T.C.S.)**
© June 12, 1998

-Inspired by the passing of a friend, not directly my own-

My grandmother knows many people, but none more special in my heart then her friend Sue. As a young vibrant single mother she struggled to raise two children on her own and instilled love, life and spirituality into the two while making it seem easy. We only connected briefly before her passing, discussing my poetry and she suggested then that I write a book. This poem keeps her living in my heart and this book is a small tribute to the love and kindness she bestowed upon me & the world.

8. "I. C. Y."

I.C.Y. people have so much stress
I.C.Y. police trip off the way you dress
I.C.Y.

I.C.Y. grandparents choose to leave no will
I.C.Y. gangs shoot and kill
I.C.Y.

I.C.Y. someone has to constantly swallow their pride
I.C.Y. so many lives end in suicide
I.C.Y.

I.C.Y. youngsters can no longer go to the park and play
I.C.Y. youth can't read, but can slay

I.C.Y., but was the price too high?
It only took my life, just to C.Y.

By: **The Crimson Spirit (T.C.S.)**
© June 1998

-Inspired while working with an Inner City Youth program-

Not one of my favorite poems, but it still deserved to be in this book. Many of our inner city youth are challenged with learning life's lessons while navigating hurdles such as gangs, drugs and financial instabilities. Broken families, hearts and spirits are also found in the pages of their already challenging book of survival. I was no different.

Drug dealers & users, love makers & abusers and other unsavory types are just a few descriptors of my immediate family. Just because you come from homes that produce more drama than any prime time TV show, does not mean you have to succumb to your influences. Stand up, get out and shine bright in your own divine light! It's not only your choice, it's your right!

9. "Deceived"

Besieged, scathed, heart now broken
Sorry as the words you've spoken
Intent unknown, precious increments
Of love, left past tense
Hollow, shallow, stabbed in the back as I wallow
Knee deep in the pit of the love that I followed

The feelings of a love left to bleed
The knowledge of a soul that's been deceived

A bell tolls in the night
Dreadful reminder of the dying light
Inside I can feel my oncoming fright
Of never again seeing the sun that shown so bright
With my last bit of strength and all of my might
I can pull myself from this hole, if I fight

The struggle of a love buried like a seed
The thoughts of a soul that was in need
The story of someone who was deceived

I hear the howl of the wind through trees
And I think of the flowering fields buzzing with bees
The darkness creeping ever so slowly
The coming of death is ever so lonely

I wish he could hear me
Or love me ever so dearly
But not now, like this
Face down bleeding in the mist

The pain of a love drowned in tears of sorrow
The fear of a soul crying for tomorrow
The life of someone who was not received
The world of a man who was deceived

If only he were true and had never gone astray
Then maybe I would not be in this ditch bleeding this way
My life for a night of sinful pleasure
Was far more important to him than any Godly measures
Eyes now closing, I find it hard to think
Blood running slowly as a spilled decanter of ink
The first ray of light from the crack of dawn
Falls softly on the hand of a man now gone

The fight of a love left to die in the night
The wisdom of a soul searching for light
The tale of someone who was misled
The realm of a man whose heart has bled
The spirit of a child that has been conceived
From the soul of a man that was deceived

By: **The Crimson Spirit (T.C.S.)**
© July 1998
Rev. July 2013

-"Deceived" an homage to Edgar Allen Poe-

I cannot remember what event(s) in my life triggered this poems creation, but once again it felt like a possession. It was as if the poem was predestined for the page and I just traced it out to make it visible to the unaided eye. At this stage in my love life I'm sure there was some type of deception from a lover or two, but nothing that could have driven me to stalk them into the night.

In hindsight it truly felt like it was a warning from the hereafter. When I dotted my last "I", I remember crying over a fictional man who had given his heart and his life for love. I remember not ever wanting to be THAT man.

10. "Where Does All the Money Go?"

Where does all the money go?
Is what we really want to know?

How can we learn about history?
When the location of all the books is a mystery
How can we learn arithmetic?
When the food in the cafeteria makes us sick

How can we do P.E.?
When there is no security
How can we learn to resist drugs and dope?
When the bathrooms have no soap
How can we graduate?
When all our schoolwork has mistakes

How can we learn computers?
When they are stolen by cocaine shooters
How can we wear uniforms?
When it is the school itself that's in need of reform

How do you expect for us to speak to the masses?
When all we know are overcrowded classes
How do you expect for us to touch the stars we're supposed to reach?
When most teachers aren't even willing to teach
How do you expect for us to celebrate school pride?
When the location of the school is the reason why our friends died

How do you expect for us to reach the top?
When the world keeps telling us to stop

But the question still remains, where does all the money go?
And that is what I really want to know

By: **The Crimson Spirit (T.C.S.)**
© June 1998

11. "Can LAUSD Handle the Schools?"

Can LAUSD handle the schools?
Make the bad kids follow the rules?

Unsafe classrooms, not enough books
Graduating, looking to the future to avoid the hooks
Of drugs, roaming the halls,
Kicking the walls,
Overcrowding,
Lack of communication with the faculty

Racial tension, gang fights and violence.
Teachers walkin' around sayin' "I'm `bout it, `bout it",
Dirty bathrooms, bad food, talkin' bout the county blues
Feeling underestimated, misunderstood, abused
No more "Say no to drugs", steppin' on bugs, burnin' the rugs,
breakin' the locks , avoidin' the cops, knockin' down pops,
gang bang, nicotine, "help us keep our campus clean",
No more school, no more books, no more teachers' dirty looks,
Insane, membrane, sex, rape it's all the same,
dress code, No Doze, just to make it anything goes,
right out the door, "she's a whore", "catch that nigga at the store",
long lines, "he's fine", keep your patience all the time,
hold up, interrupt, "I'm gon' git my jimmy sucked",
intense, high fence, "keep it up", no impotence

Stop, look and watch
Shhh.... Hear that... That's the sound of change

By: **The Crimson Spirit (T.C.S.)**
© 1998

12. "Exit"

Exit, leave me here
     Don't look back, for I have no fear

Exit, don't say good-bye
     For no matter what I hear it's all a lie

Exit, you need to leave
     For I'm not going to let you make my heart bleed

Exit, you're not wanted anymore
     For I will no longer be your battered whore

Exit, go ahead and pack
     For I'm not gonna wait for your next smack

Exit, hit the street
     For I'm tired of being stomped beneath your feet

Exit, I don't need your shit
     For I'm not going, not going to be flinching, a reflex from
          getting hit

Exit, no more excuses
     For I'm tired of all the cuts and bruises

Exit, get outta my life
     For I will no longer be your lover, babies mother or wife

     These are the things I should have said,
     no longer needed now that I'm dead

By: **The Crimson Spirit (T.C.S.)**
circa 1998

13. "Alone In The Dark"

A-gony, pain, misery and hate
L-ife now fleeting, darkness has sealed my fate
O-nly now can I find peace
N-ow that I am deceased
E-vils trickle down my arm into a pool

I-magining myself not loving a fool
N-o more thoughts of the feelings for you that I hide

T-he disappearance of light, as my head falls to the side
H-ow could you not understand?
E-ven though I tried so hard to be your man

D-ays ago I could hardly think
A-ll of that's over as my body begins to sink
R-eleasing the love of a broken heart
K-illing of a spirit that's been torn apart

The end of a love, left

Alone In The Dark

By: **The Crimson Spirit (T.C.S.)**
© June 1998

14. "I Made Love to the Devil"

Intense heat, burning my outer shell
Hot is this damnatious place called Hell
Demons and serpents all part of the fray
They laugh at the resident's pain, torture and dismay

High atop throne sits the Devil himself
Surrounded by bones of the evils he's dealt
His body was of perfection, just right in every way
No sharp nails, long horns, and tails like everyone else might say

His walk was not that of a hurried pace
His hair was kept neat, as well as his face
His skin was tanned, not red like cut meat
And he walked though the fires with no soles on his feet

As he approached, he took my hand
And through his garments I could see what made him a man
I quickly returned my eyes to his face
Only to discover on me, his eyes in the same place

A gesture was made and I was disrobed
My body now freezing from eyes that stared cold
He looked me over and seemed to be pleased
Inside he must have chuckled at all my evil misdeeds

He laid me down upon the ground
And from the mouths of every cretin there was not a sound
His first kiss, burned like fire upon my chest
I knew from that point on he would handle the rest

As he filled me, my insides burned with fire
Warm gases then lifted us up, higher and higher
High above his fiery realm, his silence broke
And I will never forget the words he spoke

His words onto me were: "This shall be my finest day."
And I thought to myself: "Who would ever think of the Devil being
gay?"
As time went on and the feelings did too
Who would think that he almost said, "I love you"?

I then awoke, thanks to my noble steed
Rubbing my head from which I bleed
I must have hit it while riding through the wood
Punishment for thinking thoughts that no mortal should

As I steadied my horse
I thought, it must have been a dream of course
And this I thought, until my garments I did part
Only to find the burned impression of lips upon my heart

By: **The Crimson Spirit (T.C.S.)**
© June 1998

-Alone In The Dark & I Made Love To The Devil-

Both poems were written in the same night one right after the other. I had never before been so inspired or moved by my own poetry that another poem just poured out right after the first. "Alone In The Dark" was one of my poetry challenges to myself. It was short yet captivating to me and as I reread it for spelling errors the other poem began to form title first, "I Made Love To The Devil".

I started imagining what was waiting for a man who had committed suicide. At first I didn't believe it would pan out, but I remember feeling so spent when I finished the last line and almost shocked myself at the "twist" ending. The poem practically wrote itself and after a few tweaks encouraged by a close friend it was completed and ready for the world to experience.

15. "In My Mind You Belong to Me"

When you are in pain,
turn to me
I will be there for you,
can't you see
No one can comfort you
like I
I feel this way and that's
no lie
Luscious angel hear my plea,
because you see in my mind
you belong to me

When the time comes and you need
a friend
I will be there for you till
the end
No one really understands
your heart
But I do, I've been there from the
very start
That's because your love is not a show
to see
And in my mind you belong
to me

I feel the words that people hold
so dear,
Will never come from your lips to
my ear
But still, I wait
Wanting to be hooked by your bait
What a shame these things will
never be
But still in my mind you belong
to me

By: **The Crimson Spirit (T.C.S.)**
© June 12, 1998

16. "Maybe If..."

Maybe if...

    We kept the campus clean,
        Then going to school wouldn't seem so mean

    We helped each other,
        Then there would be no more tears to cry from mothers

    We tried to understand,
        Then man would not need to kill another man

    We said what is on our mind,
        Then love would not be such a hard thing to find

    We held on to our dreams,
        Then things wouldn't be as hard as they seem

    We searched for hope instead of sorrow,
        Then there would be place for life tomorrow

    We cared a little more,
        Then it would be safe for children to walk to the store

    We walked in someone else's shoes,
        Then riots would not be reported on the news

    We felt for each other's pain,
        Then there would be no need for tears to fall like rain

    We focused on all the stars instead of some,
        Then no one would care "What set you're from?"

    We focused on the world's need,
        Then there would be no people hooked on speed

    We focused on space and how it's so vast,
        Then there would be no need for a lower class

    We stop giving up and really tried,
        Then no one would have to dismiss his or her pride

    We didn't knock people down to get ahead,
        Then there would be no children underfed

        Maybe if I went on like this for days,
        To show people that love pays

World Change

By: **The Crimson Spirit (T.C.S.)**
© June 12, 1998

17. "A Family Painting"

On a canvas of hues of greens and blues
Colors combine beginning the life line
Some colors are short, some tall
These colors are loved by all
Some colors are narrow, some wide
These colors inspire family pride
Which we should all feel deep inside

Some colors shine bright, some hide from the light
Some colors shy, some bold
Some colors new, some old
But when one color pales and fades away
The other colors remain to stay
The remaining colors must strive to shine
But not to hide the missing color
But in honor and remembrance to strive above all others

The dreams and wishes of the colors are only bound by the
boundaries of the frame
But that will not stop them reaching out past the framed boundaries
for a lost colors name
A family is like a painted picture
Many colors, styles, and depths
But all joined together to make a beautiful illustration
Depicting the strength and courage of a great generation

When the time comes and the colors finally reach the frame
Its hold will be broken by the strength, courage, endurance, power
and love of all the colors that came before called out by name
And in that time the colors will leave their canvas of green and blue
To start another journey free willed and anew

By: **The Crimson Spirit (T.C.S.)**
© April 26, 1999

18. "Leave My Heart Alone"

It's midnight on a Friday and I'm home alone
Contemplating whether I should page or call you on the phone
I hear your voice on the voicemail system
Spitting out your lyrical words of wisdom
My message is short, brief and to the point
Of how I want to kiss your entire body from joint to joint
As I hang up the phone, I uncontrollably exhale
Thinking of my heart that cupid's arrow has impaled
An hour passes and I lie awake in bed
Entranced by visions of you within my head
Fantasies of you fade at the ringing of the phone
My eyes tear as you say: "I want to be left alone"
Within my heart cupid's arrow burns and I feel I could die
Especially when you ask me: "How can you love me? And why?"
I could answer your question, but you would not even care
How could you love me with a love of which you are emotionally unaware?
Silence echoes over the phone line
You hang up saying: "This was not worth my time"
I cry as I sit and cradle the phone
Wishing in my head for cupid to leave my tortured heart alone
Another hour passes and the phone rings again
Your voice I hear on the other end still wanting to be friends
I realize at that point that it is not cupid who is playing with my heart
But in fact it is you who is tearing my love apart
You say: "The things I said to you were harsh..." and you want to make amends
But you also want me to know that we can never be lovers, we can only be friends
You end our call by saying: "I still love you" and I say: "I love you too"
Still in the end my heart is left torn, burning and broken in two

By: **The Crimson Spirit (T.C.S.)**
© November 26, 1999

19. "Love Bi the Hour"

Come home late from a 9 to 5
Neva thought that love would have me working over time
I throw my bag to the floor and undo my tie
As the room slowly fills with the sweet aroma of pie
I enter the kitchen and see you standing there
Our eyes meet as you give me this lustful stare
You slowly walk over to me, as if in some kinda show
Dragging your hand along the counter as you go
Gracefully you body glides into my arms
The same ones that kept you from many harms
You look up to give me a passionate kiss
I look away and my lips a complete miss
As your soft cotton candy lips grace my cheek
I think of the affair that's been going on for a week
My late nights spent away from home
Supposed to be working, but I'm not alone
Instead I'm hugging and loving a guy named Mike
Who pounds my ass with the force of an iron spike
His body is big as well as his piece
Holding and kissing me to help my shaking to cease
His touch is soft, but he is as hard as steel
His falling deep in love with me wasn't part of the deal
Now I'm standing here torn between the man and woman I love so
much
Shaking at the thought of avoiding your next touch
I take your hand and lead you to the door
Surely my love for you is worthy of more
I think my wife of twelve years should understand
Of how I could love a woman as well as a man

By: **The Crimson Spirit (T.C.S.)**
© October 1, 1999
Rev. November 2012

20. "Waking Into a Dream"

Laying in a beautiful enclosed blue canopy bed
Thinking of all the things my mother said
About love at first sight, 'bout vacations at Club Med,
'Bout getting married? Oh yeah, she gave the go ahead
Watching you make your way to my side of the bed
I playfully pull the comforter over my head
Only to have you remove my down feathered shield
You grin at my lavender silk pajamas you have worked to reveal
I step into my cotton soft house shoes as my clothes you begin to peal

The scenery quickly changes to an exquisite ballroom
And here I stand within your arms dressed as an elegant groom
I look you over as you take my hand
And I notice your Tux is a Pierre Cardin
A song begins to play
While my hips begins to sway
It's a salsa beat that attacks us at our weakest points, our feet

Our bodies move across the dance hall floor
Just as graceful and smooth as the ballroom décor
The dance floor swiftly fills with couples
Each one dancing as our body doubles
Every move we choose to display, they mimic in every way
The tempo quickens, my hold on reality slippin'
The lights and sounds blend together and the room feels like it's
tippin'
Then everything stops
You smile, a champagne cork pops

I hear the score of a familiar ballad playing
Then I hear your voice saying
Everything I want and need to hear
Ending with "I love you" and beginning with "Dear"
Your hands gently caress mine
Our eyes meet not for the first and definitely not for the last time

As our hearts began to beat a rhythmic tone
The scenery fades and suddenly were alone

A gentle wind blows and we're surrounded by Giant Red Wood
The soft grass beneath our bare feet feels so good
The moon hanging softly in a star filled sky
Reminds me of all the good times gone by
Your kiss upon my chest
Lays all my worries to rest
The love I have for you and you for me
Will keep us together for eternity
And this I know for sure
As your gentle arms bring me to the grassy floor

The love we make echo's throughout the trees
Along with the erotic screams of 'Please'
I feel a light sprinkle and a warm rain begins
Helping our lovemaking to end
I hear your moans of pleasure as you come to the point of release
And then the passion rain has ceased
My world then becomes full of your life-force
As I release I think: 'To Hell with Natures course'

Then I awaken to the sound of the radio playing that familiar melody
And rolling over to see your warm body laying next to me
Your eyes open and then you smile
Then I know that the whole relationship has been worth while
You pull me close for a kiss
One that my heart and soul would never want to miss
I feel your strong arms surrounding me
As my eyes began to tear to point where I cannot see
Then at that moment I realize that no matter how good it seems
No dream is better than my reality

By: **The Crimson Spirit (T.C.S.)**
© August 2, 1999

21. "Tears in the Dark"

The smell of cinder fills the air
As laughter turns sourly into despair
The smoldering tip of cupid's arrow that has missed its mark
As a deepening river of silent tears fall in the dark

Passions fire burns deeply in my heart
As I realize that I was cursed from the very start
Fiery embers soar into the sky
As the darkness consumes every tear I cry

My heart burst into a hellish blaze
As my soul becomes entrapped in a smoke filled maze
My torso consumed by a fire burning out of control
As the river of tears fills the darkness of my soul

Steam arises at the meeting point of salted water and flame
As my lips slowly recite over and over the sound of your name
The opposing forces battle fiercely to gain their prize
As the darkened tears drain me til I die

The battle of heated passion over sadness of sorrow
Is to hard a struggle to deal with morrow after morrow
I must extinguish the flames of passion and desire
And dam up this river of sorrow and pain, before the day my soul
expires

By: **The Crimson Spirit (T.C.S.)**
© January 26, 2000

22. "King Of Real Inspiration"

Enter into my head
Help me with the words I've said
Fill my heart with fire
Your power is what I desire
I invoke thee against thine will
For your strength, in me to fulfill
Come into my fragile soul
My hands are here to control
I can feel the weight of your stare
Your electric aura coursing through the midnight air
The ground shakes beneath me
Darkness surrounds me, now it's all I see
Falling hard onto my knees
The dark air around me begins to freeze
My body shivers after a sudden chill
Silence all around, the air goes dead still
I feel the warmth of a warm hand
I look up to see the silhouette of a man
He lifts me slowly by my chin
I could feel his power coursing within
His will too strong to resist
Overwhelming strength in his deep kiss
Hands filled with power, so much
I tremble at the slightest touch
Our souls intertwined by the force of the night
My undying love for him I can no longer fight
A tear falls
As a wolf calls
The signal of a new life
The end of his and mine the only price
Intense and unimaginable pleasure
As our bodies merge together forever

By: **The Crimson Spirit (T.C.S.)**
© January 26, 2000

23. "Visions in My Head"

Stars collide, as your lips touch mine
How I wish we could live this moment for all time
Then the ground shakes, it starts tearing at the seams
That is when I realize that this is only in my dreams
I then envision us walking in the park
A light fog rises and I notice it is way after dark
The moon is hung high in the sky
And the world seems to stop, as I look deep in your eyes
You pull me close and kiss my hand
I begin to cry because you are my man
You gently wipe a tear from my face
Then hold it close to your heart and then fling it into space
The tear streaks like a comet across the sky
As you tell me I would have no more tears to cry
Your strong arms wrap around my waist
And I find myself again staring deeply at your face
I look in your eyes and see a story of words not said
And I then again realize that this is only in my head
I close my eyes and bury my head in your chest
The scent of your body puts my heart to the test
Slowly I feel your body start to rise
And the dream slowly fades as I open my eyes
A soft glow comes over me as I sit at the edge of the bed
Enkindled by the longing visions of you in my head

By: **The Crimson Spirit (T.C.S.)**
© February 2, 2000
Rev. November 2012

24. "Rescue Me"

Reach in your hand deep into this burning sea
Reach in and please could you rescue me
For I'm drowning in this deep torrid burning hell
My arms and legs struggling to keep my head above the swell

Reach in your hand and pull me from the deep
Reach in and bring me above water to my feet
For I feel that I'm becoming very weak
My mind is beginning to give in to the eternal sleep

Reach in your hand and your power of peace
Reach in and cause the waves to cease
For I can't take this tossing and turning any more
My eyes are yearning to see the sandy shore

Reach in your hand and call out my name
Reach in and with your power these waves will tame
For I want to be in your arms again
My breath becomes short as my sinking begins

Reach in with your hand and don't waste time
Reach in and rescue the essence of my mind
For I'm in love with you and I have to let you know
My body has been longing for your sweet caress, so please take it slow

Reach in your hand into this wicked whirlpool
Reach in and rescue a drowning fool
For all this time I've waited to be saved by you
My mind not knowing that you needed saving too

Our hands meet somewhere between the air and the crashing sea
No more drowning, because your heart, soul and mind are now a part
of me
Rescued Finally

By: **The Crimson Spirit (T.C.S.)**
© February 12, 2000 Rev. 3/2012

25. "Love, Lust, Envy And Hate"

Long shadows cover our tracks as we walk along the sand
On the wings of angels my love soars as you hold my hand
Velvet lips grace my cheek
Endless whispers to my ears you speak

Longing for the heat of your touch
Understanding that I should not feel for you as such
Serpents' words of lust corrupting my will
Time and time again my body is frozen still

Entranced by the things you have and I want
Now your contentment is inferred as a taunt
Very strong envious urges to take what is yours and make it mine
You have no idea what goes on in this heart this time

After all this
No more lips to kiss
Didn't think I would ever miss

How we used to lay together
And how I thought it would last forever
That's all over now, now that you've cheated
End of our time together, you have been defeated

By: **The Crimson Spirit (T.C.S.)**
© March 25, 2000

26. "Sleep Stalker"

Silently I watch you sleep

Taking note of your breath as I begin to creep

I watch the rise and fall of your chest

As I ponder which route would be best

I figure I should come in from the side

Since it makes it easier for my hand to slide

Sharing this moment with you is a great joy

I couldn't imagine this with any other boy

Gently pulling back all the covers

Envisioning us passionately entangled as lovers

Undressing your exposed sexy body with my lusting eyes

Trembling at the thought of pulling your pants slowly past your thighs

I reach in and softly place my hand on your waist

My finger slowly searching blindly for the perfect place

Feeling my way right to your cock

I feel my own piece that is hard as a rock

Softly rubbing your thick and throbbing rod

I sort of think of myself as a powerful God

Knowing just the right amount of pressure

Supplying just the right amount of pleasure

To keep from disturbing you from your sleep

To keep your body from reaching its sexual peek

I quietly undo your fly

And marvel at the sight before my eyes

I use the opening of your boxers to release

The massive object of my next feast

Jaumonta Roberts

Licking my lips, like washing my hands before grace

I prepare myself for the dick I'm going to taste

Your round smooth head slides gracefully across my lips

As I calmly rub between my hips

Your head is in, followed quickly by the shaft

I knew by this point, this time surely was not going to be my last

I feel the wiry hairs surrounding the base

Teasing and touching, making love to my face

I could feel the pressure within me build

As my mouth your sweet flesh begins to fill

I can't take any more I have to release

I toss my head back as my shorts soak up every sticky piece

I slowly redo the clothes I unmade

And laugh at the little game that we just played

The next time we play I'm sure it will be fun

Because next time I will be sure you are awake when I'm done

By: **The Crimson Spirit (T.C.S.)**
© March 28, 2000

27. "The Date"

Wondering if you're at home alone
I call your house, but you're not at home
As the machine comes on, I hear that familiar song
The same one we were kissing to all night long
Seeing your face as I hear your voice
Knowing at that moment that I made the right choice
Remembering the nights that voice lulled me to sleep
Breaking my trance in time to hear, "Please leave a message after the beep."

Listening to the rest of the musical score
Longing to hear your deep sexy voice once more
But alas the message ends
Now what do I say? It all depends...
Do I want you to come over or do I want to go out?
Do I want to be whispering your name or do I want to shout?
I leave you a message saying meet me at my place at eight
I hang up the phone and I can hardly wait
I drive to the store and grab an expensive bottle of red wine
As I rush into the flower shop I check the time

7:15pm not a moment to waste
Have to get back to the house post haste
On the way to house I grab some soft music to play
Turning off the headlights as I enter the driveway
Put the wine on ice and prepared a romantic meal
Starting with steamed rice and ending with perfectly seasoned veal
For desert I was thinking of something a little less greasy
Like the sweet taste of you followed by the warm feeling of me going down
easy

I pull back the covers on my bed
And coat the sheets in soft rose petals, from foot to head
Lighting strawberry incense to get the house smelling just right
Showering and changing my clothes, preparing myself for the events of the
night
I was looking fabulously tight

Jaumonta Roberts

Cream Armani suit with the shoes and Kangol to match
When I saw it the store I knew this suit was all that
The clock strikes eight and I'm ready for my perfect date
No phone call saying you're going to be late
9:30pm on the clock and you're still not here
Cars drive by and out my front window I constantly peer
I pick up the phone and call your house at ten
Hoping to leave another message again
But instead I change my mind
I figure I should go and see you this time

I get in my car and refresh my cologne
Wishing to pick you up and bring you to my home
11:30pm and I'm in front of your place
But there is another car parked in your space
I go up to the door and paused before I knocked
I hear an unfamiliar voice, which alerted me to stop

I back away from the door, I can't believe my ears
I know you couldn't be cheating on me, this is worst than I feared
Putting my ear to the door, in hopes to hear some more
I wasn't prepared for what was really in store
The door opened slightly and I could clearly see your bed
I gasped at the sight of some woman's legs wrapped tightly around your head

Long polished nails trekking through your short hair
And all I could do is watch and stare
I close the door, I could not believe my eyes
I could probably understand better if it was with another guy
With all the love I gave, you were never mistreated
But it was with this woman that you cheated
I got in my car in tears and slowly drove away
Leaving behind one red rose on the hood of the car in the driveway

By: **The Crimson Spirit (T.C.S.)**
© April 18, 2000

36

28. "Why Do I Try?"

I say, "I love you"
And you say, "You do?"
I say, "I care"
You say, "I was unaware"

Why do I try?
Why do I cry?
Why do I want to die?

I look for an answer from the sky,
But time after time there is no reply

I go to church and I pray
I pray that this love for you will go away
Night after night I lay in my bed
Silently wishing that I were dead
I cry myself to sleep, it's the only way that I find peace
Waking only to find that this love for you refuses to cease

Why do I try?
Why do I cry?
Why do I want to die?

I look for an answer from you,
But time after time you don't have a clue

You have my heart
Not just an inch, but each and every part
My body reacts to your voice, your touch, and your hugs
Just the thought of you and I feel like I've been drugged
Has God truly given up on me?
Or is He just not hearing my plea?

Why do I try?
Why do I cry?
Why do I want to die?

I look for the answer deep within me,
But when I get there you are all I see

Reduced to uncontainable tears
At the thought of you being near
Cries for help that no one can hear
All because I love you and only you my dear

By: **The Crimson Spirit (T.C.S.)**
© April 22, 2000

-The inspiration for many of my love poems thus far -

Is a guy I had a secret crush on after high school. I befriended him
hoping to gain some insight as to how to win his heart and mind, but
was never successful in doing so since our desires were completely
different. He loved women and I loved him. I remember the day that I
told him how I felt about him. He laughed at first until he saw the
tears streaming down my face. He hugged me and told me that he
wished that I didn't feel that way, but also let me know that he could
never love me in the same capacity as I did him, we can be friends,
even "brothers" and we still are "bros" til this day, but I really wished
for the both of us that things could have been different. I wish we
could have enjoyed a loving, passionate friendship for all these years
of knowing each other.

I feel things in our lives would have been no less than perfect. All the
hugs, the kisses, the love, the kids, the cars, the house and vacation
homes... You can tell I thought about this a lot! I really feel he was (is)
my soul mate, just not the one I could freely date or marry. I believed
in and dreamed of love while I was with him. He made many of my
sad days turn to glad days just by being close by. If the world was less
conforming, a bit more understanding and a whole lot more loving,
we could have been together, but religion, biases and hatred all have
consumed our individual freedoms to a point where we are slaves in
our own heads, hearts and prisoners of the sexual conformities of our
bodies.

29. "Only in Silence"

Lights brightly flashing down onto the stage
And in my mind I sadly rewrite the page
Standing here, a male queen on my throne
Slowly gazing through the crowd and I know I'm not alone
Softly swaying to the musical score
Overwhelmed by the sound as I hear the audiences roar

A quartet of trumpets blaze in my ears
As I let loose my first note while fighting back tears
A drum beat rhythmically follows
This is my third concert here at the Apollo
None of these people know of the thoughts that I possess
Many have wondered, speculated or guessed
Is he straight, bi, gay or what?
Lying about all my feelings is silently driving me nuts

Singing duets with beautiful women, my vocals in the lead
Dreaming at night of a beautiful man coming to fulfill my need
Only in my mind, only in silence can I yell without anyone hearing
my screams
While walking down the red carpet as women pull on my clothes
ripping the seams
Pulling a young girl from the crowd to sing to on stage
While knowing in the lyric book of my mind there is a boy's name
written on the page

Softly singing to her while a tear runs slowly down her face
Knowing that at that moment her tears mean nothing, because my
heart is displaced
Continuing my song as she kicks and screams as security drags her
away
Singing the same song, same stage, different girl, different day

Soulfully cooing out high notes followed by deep baritones
Of a song I wrote while I was sitting in the dark, in my condo, alone
Singing a song of love, lust and hot sex in the rain
Over the roar of thousands of women and men screaming my name

Taking my final bow, I didn't want for the song to end so soon
Dreading returning back to the neatly wallpapered walls of my hotel
room

What is the purpose of success?
If you have to lie about who you are and suppress the rest

By: **The Crimson Spirit (T.C.S.)**
© July 20, 2000

-Inspired by the dreams of a close friend in the industry-

When I wrote this poem it was so farfetched to me to think that anyone could truly be successful in "the business" while being honest and open about who or how they loved. A good friend of mines is majorly talented; his voice is powerful, controlled and star worthy. I hoped along with the rest of our peers that he would find success in his dreams of stardom without having to diminish his inner "flame".

Many years later and he is still an iconic, yet local talent. I'm not sure how much of his dream was squandered by his refusal to be anything less or different then who he truly is. I am proud of him for holding his ground and not conforming to the norms of societal pressures. However, I would have also loved for the world to except him then as easy as it is for many to accept him now. I still believe in his success for later down our road of life. - R.I.P. Tracy Kennedy

30. "Undercover Lover"

Enter into my world the gay O.G.
Creepin' through LA back streets where no one can see
Saggin' jeans, red FuBu shirt and spiffy new high tops
Hat brim low, just enough to shade my eyes from the oncoming cops
Giving them the universal "Hi" sign as they roll pass
Mind on my money, my dojo and tonguing up a nice piece of ass

Steady creepin', strolling stealthily down the block
This gangsta/thug "T" can't nobody clock
Adjusting my eyes to the double flash of the headlights of a nearby car
A signal from the homies to let me know that the cops are not far
Thowin' up the "B" so that they could see
That the message was understood and received

"One-Time" was somethin' I really don't need
Especially when I have a backpack full of weed
Creepin' and shit while I'm out on parole
Slangin' this chronic while I'm out on my stroll
Strollin' again down another dark and quiet street
Jeans getting heavy weighed down by my heat

Getting to the house on time, cause I'm neva late
Grabbing the best flowers planted at the foot of the gate
The family is gone, the windows of the front house are all black
I open the gate and go to my niggas place in the back
Get to the door and use our secret knock
Listening to my baby as he fumbles with the locks

The door opens up and there he is
Just the sight of him almost fills my shorts full of jiz
I give him the flowers and he gives me a hug
I stand in the doorway entranced by his beautiful mug
My arms wrap around his sculpted bod
As his hands rubs places that he finds very fond
Kissing his lips as hands fall between hips

Jaumonta Roberts

The door closes behind us
And I break our passion filled kiss of lust

Taking his large hand and gently leading him to the couch
Unleashing my piece and sending it straight to his mouth
Soft lips sliding smoothly down my shaft
The thought of the homies seeing us now, almost makes me laugh

His left hand caressing every crevice of my abs
His right hand undoing my belt,
letting my pants fall revealing my muscled ass
His left hand slides slowly down the crack and he inserts a finger
If my girl found out about this we'd probably end up on Jerry Springer

I feel the pressure in me build and I don't want to bust in his throat
But before I could pull away,
his finger goes deeper and his tonsils I do coat
Warm surges of sextasy flow from my center and out to my hand
As his lips hold tight to my piece like a moist cock band

My knees give out and I fall back onto the couch
Forcing him to release my piece from his moist mouth
Kissing me everywhere as he positions himself over me
The world is set on mute,
then it just falls away and his face is all that I see

Our lips lock and off goes our socks
Our hands meet and our pants are knocked off by our feet
Our thighs press and there is nothing left to undress

A wet coat of KY is generously applied
And with a glove he puts all his love inside
Rhythm in all his motions, going in and out
Passionate kisses caressing my neck and mouth

Deeper and deeper his love impales
I reach for his back and wish I had nails
To carve into his back all the things I would say
If his tongue was not ravishing my mouth this way

These words could truly explain how I feel
And I'm sure his love goes deeper than the thick nine-inch piece that he deals
His dark skin should have a sign "Slippery When Wet"
As sweat pours as we moan and groan like the night we first met

His life force fills the sheath in multiple warm waves
As we hold on to each other like two runaway slaves
Feeling the deep pulsating throbs of his softening rod
Slowly simmering in warm salty sweat under the watchful eyes of God
Looking down on two brown bodies harmoniously intertwined

Loving each other in heart, spirit, body and mind
Morning sunlight peeking through the window as we shower
Lathering each other up bodies slipping and sliding for hours
A loving kiss behind closed doors before I go
Back out on the streets, ready to make some more dough

By: **The Crimson Spirit (T.C.S.)**
© August 8, 2000

-Inspired by a crush on a "Hood" boy-

This poem was written on a legal pad and took about a week to write (about the length of the crush). It started as a dream of what I envisioned loving a guy who had a serious gang mentality would be like. You know we all want the "bad" boy until we actually get him and realize that "bad" is in no way "good". After engaging my "bad" boy and listening to his litany of issues ranging from "baby mama's" to "Hood" days and him confessing a "like" for me, I thought that this could be my chance at "Thug Love".

It turned out to be a lesson in how women (and men) get used & abused in the name of love. He stole pieces of my heart along with my money, my electronics, my trust and most precious my time. Through time we are still associates to this day and he apologized for his past actions, but he knows he will never have that opportunity with me again. Real thugs have little or no capacity to love. They only love what they can control and destroy anything that they cannot tame.

31. "Help"

My eyes I can no longer trust
Deceiving me into this nightmare of lust
Sex with a man I do not love
Dark clouds obscure the star filled sky above
His face is cold and his eyes uncaring
Inside it feels like it is at the devil that I am staring

When will I be set free?
When will someone come to rescue me?

If eyes are the windows into the soul
Then his soul is barren, corrupt and cold
I want to be free and I want to escape
But I feel that it's been too long and now it's too late

How long before this time will past?
How long will my torture last?

I cry all day and fight all night
I damn my heart for not giving me sight
To see what pain was at the end of this road
But instead letting this tragic story unfold
Lured away from the one man I truly loved
Only to have my love clipped and caged like a wild dove
Waiting to be set free
Waiting for the chance to be in my old tree

Where is the love of my old tree?
Where is the one that is familiar to me?

Memories corrupted by words of deceit
In my mind over and over your name I repeat
Will my imprisonment ever end?
Or will I be forced to love him or continue to pretend

Why does my world have no sun?
Why can't I remember when all this begun?

If there is a God, please can you help me
Help me get back to my old tree

My body is tired and my heart is weak
My voice is gone I can no longer speak

What part of my life did I go wrong?
What will I return to after being gone so long?

So I pray for you to pull me trough
Because I feel that no one has the power but you

By: **The Crimson Spirit (T.C.S.)**
© October 12, 2000

-Inspired by a wrong turn on the avenue of love-

Though this poem (and the two that follow) is/are a bit of an exaggeration of what really happened. Parts of it relate to the state of mind I was in being torn between two hearts. I was actively dating a guy who seemed at the time distant or just a bit too busy for "us". Then by chance I befriended another guy who came on very strong really quickly. I recall telling him in the beginning that I was dating someone and he seemed to understand and kept things friendly. I was running between the two for about a month or so before the second guy made an ultimatum in the middle of sex. You should never agree to anything while participating in the art of love making. I then distanced myself from the first guy who didn't seem to notice until I was already a month into the new relationship.

A month turned into a year, a year into 3 years. Many ups and downs, break ups & make ups, but through it all I learned lessons about myself that I never knew. Found new strength in places I never looked and discovered that not all love is REAL love. Yes he loved me, but more so it felt as if he wanted to possess me, devising situations to show me off to his friends and family whenever possible. Then finally I had my fill. I couldn't take another bite of a lie that I force fed myself daily, "This can work". It became "work", smiling when I really wanted to cry. Kissing a man who I couldn't fully love; while at the same time missing another man who I thought never fully loved me. Forcing my heart to live a lie, when I knew another bite of the poisoned apple would cause me to die.

32. "Sleepless Nights"

Sleeping on the edge of my bed every night
Wishing for your arms to hold me tight
Can't close my eyes to get some sleep
Thinking of how you touched my body deep
Your sweet, unique, mannish, urban flavor
Is the one I can't live without and constantly savor
Enjoying your rippled body as you lay on top
Giving me a deep pulsating love that won't ever stop
Kiss and hug, hug and kiss
Just to be near you is pure insatiable bliss
Over and under the sheets we unite
Waiting for this moment to come every night

Silently sitting and staring at my bedroom walls
Listening to the sound of my heart as it calls
Out for love that can only be provided by you
Hoping and praying you feel the same way too

Moonlight softly glowing overhead
As I hold myself rocking on the edge of the bed
Where did I lose it? How did I lose it all?
I close my eyes as a river of tears begins to fall
You are my world, my soul, the one reason that to this life that I hold
Why have I waited so long and why were you not told?

Dreams slowly becoming faded memories
Lack of sleep draining all my energies

By: **The Crimson Spirit (T.C.S.)**
© July 16, 2001

33. "In Your Bed"

In your bed
Where you lay your tormented head
You will not find any peace
Until the lies you told discontinue and cease
Tossing and turning all night
Cussing and swinging like you were in a fight
Running scared in fear for your life
Sleepless nights are only the beginning of the price
Never again will you dream of happy times
Never again will you have dreams of the loving kind
The darkness of your room
The low glow from the moon
The undeniable fear of an oncoming doom
That shows no signs of ending soon
This is the world you have created
This is the life for you that has been fated
All night you keep running
But the darkness is ever so cunning
You can't escape
The dark strings of fate
They wrap around your neck like an invisible noose
Clawing at the tight treads trying to break loose
Succumbing to your own dismay
Never again to see the light of day
Without lies your sorry ass has nothing left to say
You feel fear as your soul goes down the other way
Why did you do what you did?
Pseudo friend with the knife behind your back you hid

By: **The Crimson Spirit (T.C.S.)**

© February 14, 2002

34. "Truly Blessed"

You should know that you are truly blessed,
in putting my mind to the test

I have sought out the secret of the riddle you haveth placed
before me
And the results below is what you shall see

I had to consult with runes unknown
To give to you the vision of what must be shown

I had to reach up to touch angels
To get you this parchment that was ever so mangled

With demons encircling my feet,
I had to get you the documents that you seeked

Through storms of spirits mist and boulders that fell like hail
I knew that for you I must succeed and prevail

I stayed strong, while wading waist-deep in the bubbling bog,
just to hand you this sacred log

And what do I want in return at my journeys end?
I just want you to remain just as you have and always been,

MY TRUE FRIEND

By: **The Crimson Spirit (T.C.S.)**
circa 2004, rev. 06/2012

35. "Life Lessons"

World, world what are we coming to?
When a man can't walk down the street wearing red or blue?
And we can't tell our lover that this cough is more than the flu?

How many times a day, do we jeopardize our lives this way?
Not knowing, not knowing that there is hope, just hold fast to that
rope
And I can pull you up above to a place of true love and reason
Where joy comes every day and not just during the holiday season
Where is this place? And does it sound too good to be true?
Well the place is real and resides in you

Where there is hope, you have no room for dope
When you have people who care, you have no room for despair
Surround yourself with positive faces, and find yourself in positive
places

Find within yourself the will to live and the power to give
Forget about all those sunny days from the healing light that you hid
I know and understand the fear you have inside
I too had those feelings that caused me to hide
But then I sought help from the world outside
With my friends and family affirming my pride

No more believing my life was now doomed
No more sleepless nights by fear consumed
No more beating yourself mentally with verbal insults
No more saying "I'm Positive" and fearing negative results

Living, this time for real, no more outer layers of BS to peal
Carried along by an unforeseen force
Down a long and uncharted course
Never knowing what is waiting just round the bend
Never ever wanting your journey to end

What is it that you most cherish and desire?
What is it that sets your soul on fire?
Those things you can still acquire
Don't give up and give in, the devil is a liar
Don't douse your flame before it has a chance to burn
Don't cash in that check for your blessings, you have more to earn
There are still many life lessons to be taught and to be learned

When traveling down the tunnel of life, what will be your final stop?
Will you have a life of poverty or will you soar to the top?
Will you have love, happiness, and a mission to please?
Or will you be sick, weak and riddled with disease?
The choices are yours and mine
Now give yourself a moment to think, this is your time

By: The Crimson Spirit (T.C.S.)
circa 2005

36. "Thin Line"

LoVe

What would you do if you were in love?

Love makes you do silly things
Like buy a red convertible and fill it with ruby rings
Like a tight embrace during a private concert while Luther sings
Like sitting at the movies sharing popcorn and other tasty things
Like the warm feeling that loving someone truly brings

Laying in the bed with your head in between my legs
What you know about that can of freak, I'm going to open up a
couple of kegs
I love being with you, the two of us are such freaks
We can just keep going and going till we both start to leak
Underneath the sheets kissing and freakin' till dawn and then some
And you always make sure I get my nut before you come

But where does the love go?
What happens when the currents of love no longer flow?
Why is it so difficult for a man to let his real feelings show?
You ask me if I still love you and I just don't know

We used to kiss in the morning and come home from work at the
same time
You used to hold me, caress me and tell me "Baby you're fine"
You used to take us out to exclusive restaurants so we could dine
You used to order lavish entrees, desserts and crystal glasses of wine
You used tell me you loved me forever and will always be mine

But when does the love end?
When is the time you have to call your friends?
And be like: "Girl, my man is cheating what do you think I should
do?"
"I think me and my man are going to be through"
And she be like: "There is more fish... well in your case, meat in the
meat locker"

And you be like: "I think that bitch he is cheatin' with I think I can
cold clock her"
Then she laughs, and you laugh and then we laugh together
But you still sittin' in the house knowing you don't feel any better

Drinking beer and watching games on my couch
When in the hell did you become such a slouch?
Sitting over there with your hand down your pants losing your figure
Whatever happened to my above average nigga?
It must have been all the soul food I put on your plate?
Or could it be that other bitch's period is late?
With love and trust I took faith in your ebony words
And the thought of you and a woman wasn't far from absurd
But like they say, it's the late bitch that looses the "bird"
Humph, but I'm not going out like that, fuck what ya heard

HaTe

So now you creeping with some chick behind my back
And I got proof, my home girl got a picture of you two in the sack
Bumpin' and grindin', moanin' and groanin', slobbin' and spittin'
Damn man, I wish it was me that was hittin'
Crappy, nappy weave, red fake nails, just another tired ass hoe
And I bet you money under that horse hair the bitch has a teenie
weenie afro

From the mouths of men lies and games, lies and games
Are all these niggas are just the same?
What ever happen to: "You fuck with me, you stuck with me"
Or are those days just faded memories in this guy's history
I still remember those days, out playing with the boys
And you know they all cried when some else played with their toys
But here I am feeling like a toy myself
And right now I'm ready to be played with by somebody else

Now he says I have to go out of town for this convention
But I know the real reason for his expedition, Hell, I just use my male
intuition

We been together for four years and this is your first fib
What do you think I still wear a baby's bib?
If you feed me spoonfuls of shit, please could you at least have the
decency to sugar coat it

Now I've seen all the movies from "Waiting to Exhale" to "Misery"
But if you keep this shit up, you yourself will end up like a murder
mystery
Oh but did you know two REALLY can play this game?

And I can't remember one nigga' that could leave me after one night
yet alone almost four years of screaming my name

Someone told me that eatin' ain't cheatin', but I don't do tossed
salads
I want a nigga to give it to me like a bitch in the Swan Lake Ballad
Legs spread wide, what a nice place for a dick to hide
Sexy slow music playing, while the canopy over the bed is swayin'
Holding my thighs, lifting me up, holding on to the canopy rails just
to get a nut
Sex is always best when it's powered by revenge
And this is two times better, 'cause I'm with your best friend

Now there he goes jumpin' out the window holding his clothes
And you standing in the doorway with my gun to your nose
Yeah nigga I did it, I let your best friend hit it
And you thought that nigga was straight, but I felt the boi was down
from the gate
So here we stand, me with my gun in my hand
Staring coldly at a guy I would love to still have as my man.

Everyone knows that there is a thin line between love and hate,
but it is one of the most important things we leave up to fate.
And if you wait too long to find a mate
You might find yourself too old and maybe too late

By: **The Crimson Spirit (T.C.S.)**
March 9, 2005

37. "You Are"

You are the headache in the middle of my daydream
You are that annoying little kid that wants to be seen

You are that bad memory buried deep in my past
You are that stray thought that makes me cum to fast
You are that smell that builds up underneath your kitchen sink
You are that red sock that turns all your whites to pink

You are that time it rained and I had no umbrella
You are that vision of when I walked in
on my man and anotha fella

You are that track on my favorite
CD that constantly skips
You are that sweet exotic fruit that
20 minutes later has swollen my lips

You are that dog that caused me to swerve into another car
You are the reason this poem has gotten this far
You are the epitome of all the bad things that have been done to me
You are that man in the mirror I see

By: **The Crimson Spirit (T.C.S.)**
© April 14, 2006 Rev. August 3rd, 2012

38. "Seed of Love"

I planted a seed of love in your garden
I planted it in the spot where the ground has hardened
I planted a seed of love and I hope that you have room
I planted a seed of love and I can't wait for that love to bloom
I planted a seed of love for you to see
What all my love can be for you and me

I planted a seed of love that day by day is growing
I planted a seed of love that only just now has begun showing
I planted this seed with the strength my mother gave to me
I planted this seed with the tools my father passed down, you see
I planted this seed in hopes that one day it will become a tree
To one day shade and protect us from the worlds adversities

Beneath this tree I want us to grow old
Beneath this tree I want our happiness to unfold
Beneath this tree we will find shelter from the cold
Beneath this tree I want our stories to be told
Gazing at the stars from beneath our tree
I want our souls to become one and then set free

By: **The Crimson Spirit (T.C.S.)**
© May 8, 2006

39. "The Burning Fire of Desire"

Inside my soul there is this fire

Burning for you, it's my desire

Uncontrollable is the fury of its flames

But there is no heat because your lack of passion is to blame

My soul is aflame with a fire that burns cold

A flame that grows even colder without you in my arms to hold

How did you come to torture my soul this way?

Igniting it with a cinder from your lips when you kissed me that day

Ever since the flame has been growing

Ever since reaching for you without me knowing

Standing alone in the dark of night

With your flame within me burning bright

The slow freezing of my heart makes me want to fight

Fight for you cause that is what I feel is right

But that won't make you come back to me to quell this freezing light

And that is only the beginning of my plight

This flame is growing and going beyond my skin

Reaching and seeking to pull someone in

But I have to protect the world from your freezing flame

And hope someday someway your flame will be tamed

Till then I have to keep my distance from those enticed by the light

For fear of freezing the heart of my next Mr. Right

Tears form frozen streams down my face

That collect into a pool of sorrow I carry below my waist

Maybe one day after all these lessons are learned

I will be ready for a love that really burns

By: The Crimson Spirit (T.C.S.)
© June 16, 2007

40. "Love No More"

Behind this door is not what you're looking for

Cause love don't live here anymore

I had a hard time getting my last love out

If I let you in you will see some of his misplaced shit all about

Pictures of our coupling all facing the walls

Answering machine is full from me avoiding his calls

The carpet is semi moist from my falling tears

His clothes all piled up in the corner like I haven't washed in years

You would have to excuse the house if it stinks

I have dirty dishes filling my kitchen sink

Every plate contains a memory of how we were just last week

Starting with Sunday's dinner of love and ending with the ones where we didn't speak

My living room holds mixed memories of my man

Cause this is the place, on that day, he made his last stand

It's also the place we cuddled on the couch on cold Saturdays

The place where we watched the Travel Channel planning our weekend getaways

The space on the love seat where you fucked that boy from yo' hood

A bloody spot on the carpet where you sucker punched me good

Every day I work to make my way past all that you would see

But every step in any direction is just like an eternity

My bathroom is littered with all his bottles of cologne

How I wish this love of him would just go and leave me alone

His wash towel is neatly folded along the top of the shower door with care

This was one of his secret signs that he wanted to have sex in there

The smudges on the door from our last encounter that lasted hours

One day soon I will gain the strength to go in there and scour

Entering my room and I tremble while looking at the bed

Remembering the many time he left me there sexually full and fed

His clothes all over the floor from me emptying out his dresser drawers

Tiny pages scattered all about from his little black book of whores

Secrets that lie, why do we keep all our true feelings deep inside

Never owning up to all that we truly hide

Falsely living as a boyfriend but always fucking another nigga in the end

My love was given to him without a reference point

Now no longer my lips, will his kisses anoint

I had been murdered in an instant

By a love that is no longer existent

My head spins as I envision our torrid end

Anger, loneliness, misery, darkness and despair

Are all filling the place in my heart where his and my love once shared

Now love is banging on my door trying to get within

But I won't, just won't let love in

I don't want to give love another chance to begin, or win

I don't want love no more

If you came for love then you're really at the wrong door

Now I'm not saying I'm changing ways to be hard core

I just know that I don't want love no more

After years of waiting on love to come through that door

I'm tired of love leaving my heart sore

So to you, to love... I lock my door

By: **The Crimson Spirit (T.C.S.)**
© June 21, 2007

41. "In the New Year"

In the New Year I will show no fear

I will cherish the memories of those who are no longer here

I will be stronger in mind, spirit, and heart

I will no longer give in to opposition before I even start

I will be a voice to those who have none

I will strive harder to leave no days work undone

I will be a better friend, brother and lover to all

I will put full effort into life's projects no matter how small

I will pay more attention to my health and wellbeing

I will be more calculating in my decisions instead of just agreeing

I will learn what it means to have a real friend

I will know when someone's usefulness has come to an end

I will become better at distinguishing lies from the truth

I will strive to be more influential in the lives of youth

I will be all these things and more

and it is only the beginning of what is truly in store

Strive to make 2008 great and eradicate all your dead weight

Stay blessed, stay true and know that you have angels watching over
you

By: **The Crimson Spirit (T.C.S.)**
© January 7, 2008

42. "Passion Marks"

Was it because my love of you was so sweet that it tasted tart? That your jaws locked and you gave me passion marks?

Or was it 'cause you thought that your love was so good that it was considered art. That's why you always leave me with visible passion marks?

Or maybe I should have known that you were dangerous from the very start. 'Cause I know I'm in danger for letting you get so close to my heart and letting you leave passion marks

Over and under you I try to keep in mind that your bite is far worse than your bark, but still I willfully succumb to your voracious passion mark

And we never make love under the covers or in the dark. Is that so you can skillfully plot your next passion mark?

And once we get started can't anything tear us apart, especially when your lips are seared to my skin and you're leavin' a passion mark.

Kissing you all over is only where it starts, but I know before were done your going to leave your lasting passion mark

By: **The Crimson Spirit (T.C.S.)**
© March 13, 2008

43. "Lost Love"

I had a thought today that reminded me of you

and I started crying I didn't know what to do.

The day was going good for me then this left me feeling blue

I'm still realizing somewhere deep inside I still love you

You don't have to do anything special for me

Cause when I think of love, you are all that I see

You touched my heart in such an everlasting way

That nothing can force me to forget no matter how many days

Nightmares of my losing you disturbing my inner peace

Missing your kiss that would make my troubles cease

Your hands, your fingers missing your soft touch

Can't believe it's been over a year and I still miss you this much

You're only a phone call away

But if I called you, what would I say

I know thoughts of me don't cause troubles in your day

But I just can't wish my love for you away

And if I could I don't think I would

Cause I can't believe there was ever a love this good

Lost love, you know who you are...

I knew it on that first night, we talked for six hours in your car

By: **The Crimson Spirit (T.C.S.)**
© March 24, 2008

44. "Love/Prey"

Love preyed on by soulless hearts

Never quite sure of when it starts

It's a slow drain, love bleeding from the inside part

Fear lurks just outside Loves door

The fear of not knowing love no more

Suddenly the door is kicked in

Allowing entry of three strange friends

Fear enters first brandishing a devilish grin

He has been itching for this assault to begin

He's followed by Pain who carries two blades just for thrills

But he's only there to make Love hurt for he does not have the power to kill

Death then enters bringing with him an undeniable chill

He commands Fear to take hold of Love while Pain readies his blades

With a glance he commands Pain to slice till Loves vibrant color fades

Soon the carpets are thick and wet from Loves life draining to the floor

Death leans in and gives a kiss while snapping Loves neck to love no more

By: **The Crimson Spirit (T.C.S.)**
© May 11, 2010

45. "Him"

I was lost for months in thoughts of love for you
Then it struck me like a drop of rain from out the blue
Sent a chill down my spine that almost made me lose my mind
Chasing illusions of love for all this time
Talking to myself when I thought I was talking to you
Never knew you were taking all my words as untrue

I'm stressin' over all the lessons my heart should have learned
Can't stop weeping, can't rest when I'm sleeping and writing checks
on love you haven't earned
After so much soul searching I'm wondering if it's not me that is
causing our end
And even though things seem aloof right now I still want you to be
more than just my friend
Three weeks went by with me wondering why you were no longer by
my side
Three weeks of uncontrollable tears that only served to fuel my fears
Three weeks I waited with tears unabated for a love that I thought was
fated

A life without you doesn't feel like life at all
But the higher I jump, the higher your wall
Sadness slowly filling the crevices of my soul
What was once warm memories are starting to turn cold
Yet I still hang on to my phone hoping you will call
Never knew I was so high on love until the fall

After a failed attempt to drown myself in a sea of sorrow

A vivid vision gave me hope for a new tomorrow

A tomorrow full of laughter, smiles and joy

A tomorrow filled with love from a man and not a mere boy

A tomorrow filled with love that will last

A tomorrow unhindered by a hidden past

Never again will I lie in my bed and silently cry

Never again will have to wonder or ask why

He will fulfill and love me in so many ways

That I will abandon my calendar and lose track of days

Our love will empower us both to continually grow

Our love will shine so bright we couldn't help but let it show

He will be for me and I will be for him

I will cater to his every whim

This vision brings me serenity like a good gospel hymn

Then I open my eyes and see you and wonder.... Are you Him?

In life there will come times of illusion, confusion and delusion, but
through it all know and trust in your wisdom to provide the solution,
resolution and finally a conclusion

By: **The Crimson Spirit (T.C.S.)**
July 2010

46. "Living Without My Heart"

Had a talk with my heart the other day
Wasn't quite prepared for what my heart was going to say
I was told my love for you is slipping away
I was more than just shocked, I was placed in a state of dismay

Never would I dream of a time
When you would no longer be mine
Tossed out of my life like an old valentine
My knees get weak and I can't even walk a straight line

What would I do in my life without you?
Lost and alone in my room hoping for a break through
Any chance I would have at romance without you
Would be like looking for answers without a clue

Can't face the thought of waking up
Can't even find the strength to "Give A Fuck"
Dreams fade into memories out of time and out of luck
Unable to move forward, too afraid to look back, my world, my life is
stuck

So now I have to choose between my heart and my man
And I choose my man 'cause the heart just don't understand
He loves me or he loves me not is not the case
I know this cause I can read his love all over his face

So now I'm down to the hardest part
Trying to figure how long I can live without my heart
I know of machines that can keep your blood clean
Now one placed inside someone's chest is something I have never
seen

But something has to be done
I can't know love if my heart holds none
I ask for guidance from The Father, The Spirit & The Son
Because what I am going to do next cannot be undone

I readied the sharpest blade from my kitchen drawer
To dig out this heart that cannot love my man no more
I know that it's crazy and there is no way it will work as I count down
from four
I just can't imagine what he thought as he came through the door

But he rushed me just as the knife was about to kiss its mark
Knocking me to the floor with our faces just inches apart
His eyes teared up as he asked me "why?"To which I had no remark
Unable to explain how I would die without him, so I would try living
without my heart

By: **The Crimson Spirit (T.C.S.)**
© March 3, 2011

47. "In Only One Night"

In only one night... you did so many things that have never been done
right
Morning comes and I dread rolling over to the most disparaging sight
The empty spot where you would be sleeping that has been vacant too
many nights
If I would have only known that soft kiss from you that morning
Would be my last, followed by weeks of sobbing and mourning

If that morning I would have pulled you back into bed
Convinced you to stay with me while pulling the covers up over our
heads
Caressing you all over while repeating to you all the words just last
night you said
When you left I thought I was imagining this overwhelming feeling of
dread
Never imagined that you would forever be lost to me since you're
dead

Shaking off the weird feelings and pulling myself to my feet
Pulling off all the covers from the bed and then removing all the
sheets
Hearing the rain slowly falling tapping along the roof making a
soothing beat
Feeling an oncoming chill as I turn the thermostat to bring some heat
Tossing all the bedding into the wash to get out last night's many
skeets

Grabbing a warm cup of coffee from the pot you made before I woke
Sipping on the brew to knock off some of this chill taking care as not
to choke
Watching the morning news and giggling at the news anchors timely
jokes
The camera cuts to an accident of two cars that collided on a freeway
that was soaked
Your car twisted and mangled in the wreckage as my cup falls and into
many pieces, broke

So many tears that rushed down my face
Each one faster than the one before as if they were in a race
Holding myself tightly to keep from shaking as I began to pace
Not knowing what to do next, can't think my thoughts are lost to
space
I throw on something quick, grab my cell and rush from my place

As I drive to the scene of the accident I think to call your mom to tell
her the news
When she answers I can't speak through tears, but she knows
something is wrong by just the nonverbal cues
Where is my baby she asked and I tell her what I seen from the
helicopters birds eye views
She sobs, she sighs and she prays for every Sunday she sits in the first
row of pews
She tells me to be at peace because she knows that the Lord felt you
have paid your dues

Shaken awake by her strength, I wipe my tears and make my way to
where you are
As I approach I can see the smoke plume lofting from the smashed up
cars
I see the flash of lights from the emergency vehicles and I know I'm
not far
I barely stop before I hop from my car as I run up the embankment
like a track star
Screaming while being held back by officers as your lifeless body is
removed from your car

By **The Crimson Spirit (T.C.S.)**
© November 3, 2011
Rev. May 11, 2015

48. "The Debate"

Spent all night debating on love
With no solution given, I'm awaiting a sign from above
Death is contemplating while I drown in a pool of tears from a dove
While standing at the edge I grow tired from anticipating one good
shove
Nonsense made while working on relating, cause I am at a loss for
words to speak of
My love falls short of hitting its mark, my hands were trembling from
the very start an incision was made and life's blood now drains out
from my heart...

By: **The Crimson Spirit (T.C.S.)**
© January 11, 2012

-Giving Thanks-

If you made it this far into my book I truly thank you for your interest
and hope that something moved you more so than just wanting a
secondhand glimpse into the tragic depiction of my love life and parts
therein. These poems are for the most part a chronological collection
of how my love was planted, nurtured, loved and then plucked and
thrown away once the beauty began to fade. I am not saying that it
was all tragic, but tumultuous is a much better word for it. I feel as if
my entire adult life has been spent trying to gain from love what I put
into it. In the end it feels like all I got from it was prose & pain,
which might be the title of my next book!

Once again I thank you for your interest and also for your support. I
look forward to the next time you take the time to walk in my mind.

49. "How Can"

How can you love someone with a cold heart?
How can you fix what is not only broken, but ripped apart?
How can you imagine a future with someone who can't figure where
to start?
How can you show someone the light when they are completely
enthralled by the dark?
I have asked myself these questions over and over again
Only to come to the point where we must try to just be friends
How can you be friends with someone you really love and you only
want love in return?
How can you forgive and forget when everything they remember
continues to burn?
How can you gain someone's trust, when they refuse any credit that
you feel you've earned?
How can you show them that you can change for the better, when
they won't even give you a turn?
All this I ask and more, but to what avail? I thought that true love
would always prevail
Only this time it seems as if my true love has failed
How can you mend a gap that seems miles wide on either end?
How can you abandon love and attempt to still remain friends?
How can you break up to make up, but still leave no room to make
amends?
How can you expect me to stay open-minded and flexible when you
are unable to bend?
Around in circles our debates, arguments and discussions transcends
All the while our trust for one another continues to descend
I know I love you, but I'm unclear if you even love yourself
I want to move forward in our love and deny love from anyone else
I want to love you again and have you love me back in the same way
I want for you to trust in the strength of love that will never ever go
away

By: **The Crimson Spirit (T.C.S.)**
© March 12, 2012

70

50. "God Speaks"

God speaks from the mouths of bums
God speaks when there is no sun
God speaks when the healing is done
God speaks where children have fun

God sends love through a hug from a stranger
God sends angels disguised as friends to help with anger
God sends music in the form of birds on top of a manger
God sends help when His children are in grave danger

God listens when times get rough
God listens when you think you've had enough
God listens when you feel weak, but need to be tough
God listens when you can't see beyond the small stuff

God loves when you trust in Him and stop believing in "them"
God loves when you sing His praise in gospel hymns
God loves when you give into His every whim
God loves when you open your heart entirely to Him

God heals you after your many heart breaks
God heals you after you made multiple mistakes
God heals you when you feel the pain is too much to take
God heals you when you find yourself poisoned by the snake

God doesn't ever prejudge us by our sins big or small
God doesn't ever punish us no matter how far the fall
God doesn't ever stop he breaks down every wall
God doesn't ever give up on His children, He loves us all

By: **The Crimson Spirit (T.C.S.)**
© March 26, 2012

ABOUT THE AUTHOR

Jaumonta Roberts, known in the poetry circuit as The Crimson Spirit or T.C.S. for short, was born in Los Angeles, California. The eldest of his parents children, but raised congruently by his mother and grandmother who loved him exceedingly. He graduated from Alain LeRoy Locke High School in South Central L.A., where he began writing poetry in the tenth grade. Without any recognized poetic influences, he draws his inspiration from life, love and learned lessons from his high school teacher Ms. DeShay, his first mentor and motivating spirit.

His first book "The Colors of Love: Poetry of The Crimson Spirit", is an anthology of poems from his perspective as a young man dealing with sexual identity during an era when the voices of the LGBTQ community was crying out for equality and respect worldwide.

Inspired by years of employment within a domestic violence intervention agency, Jaumonta believes that "Despite how far we fall… there is always a way back up!" This book is inspirited by our "rainbow" youth who have been rejected by family and abandoned by systems put in place to maintain the "status quo" which often is determined by those far removed from the practices and policies that they enforce. His desire is to unify a divided world through his poetry and at the same time lend a voice to those who feel they have none.

Lastly, Jaumonta hopes that his poetry may inspire other gifted and hidden voices of the "rainbow" to allow their true colors to shine in the light and love of a world that may still not be quite ready for true change.

When not writing or performing his spoken word, Jaumonta is an avid gamer, network engineer, and domestic violence intervention advocate.

He currently resides in Los Angeles, CA.